[FRONT COVER PHOTO]

THE CATHEDRAL SPIRES, resembling European cathedrals, point to their maker in

God's Country, the beautiful Black Hills. (JOHN A. SUNDBY)

[BACK COVER PHOTO]

ROSE LIGHT rakes the relief of buttes in the Badlands. (JOHNNY SUNDBY)

DEDICATED TO:
Kathy and Bobby Sundby

SPECIAL THANKS TO:
Paul & Carol Niemann
OF RUSHMORE PHOTO & GIFTS, INC.
OF RAPID CITY, S.D.
FOR MAKING THIS BOOK POSSIBLE.

Distributed by
DAKOTA SKIES PHOTOGRAPHY
4780 Easy Street
Rapid City, South Dakota 57702

Printed in Korea
For Terrell Publishing Company 0994197

PHOTOGRAPHY BY JOHNNY SUNDBY & JOHN A. SUNDBY
All rights to the photography are reserved by Johnny Sundby of Dakota Skies Photography
4780 Easy Street
Rapid City, South Dakota 57702

PHOTO CAPTIONS BY JILL SUNDBY

ISBN 1-56944-065-4

IN

GOD'S COUNTRY

A Collection of Photographs of the Black Hills & Badlands

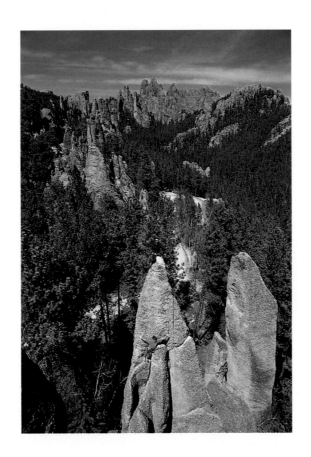

BY JOHNNY SUNDBY & JOHN A. SUNDBY

THE remnants of an after-
noon thunderstorm roll
past the stark Badlands west
of Cedar Pass Lodge.

THE waters that shroud these
Spearfish Canyon walls were named
for their likeness to a bride's veil,
Bridal Veil Falls.

THE Eye of the Needle threads
the evening sky.

THE Black Hills soften to shades
of gray with each successive ridge.

Johnny Sundby

SYLVAN LAKE, actually a reservoir

constructed for a resort in 1891,

mirrors clouds on a summer day.

I N the fall, Spearfish Canyon

displays its subtle splendor.

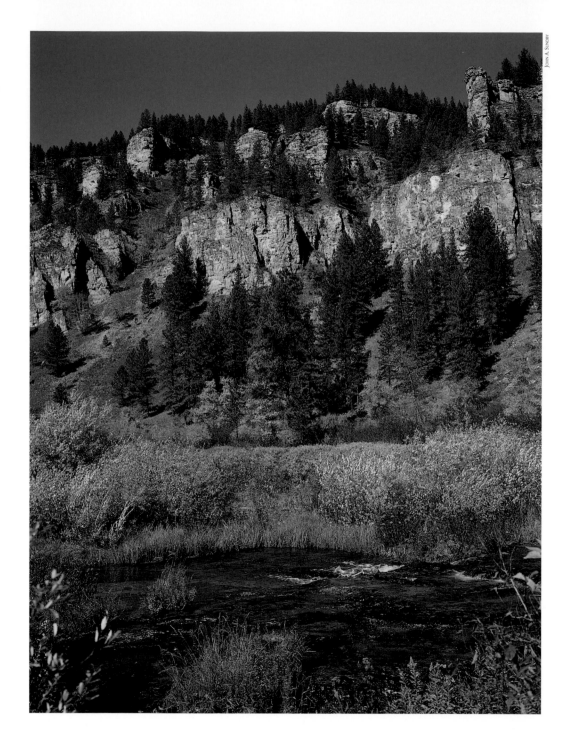

THE setting sun burnishes Pactola Reservoir, named for the mining camp which once thrived at its bottom before the dam was finished in 1956 to hold water for the Rapid City area.

JOHNNY SUNDBY

JOHNNY SUNDBY

WHEAT ripens in amber waves of grain near the small town of Scenic.

PEACEFUL Rapid Creek turned into a raging river on June 9, 1972, killing 238 people in and around Rapid City.

JOHN A. SUNDBY

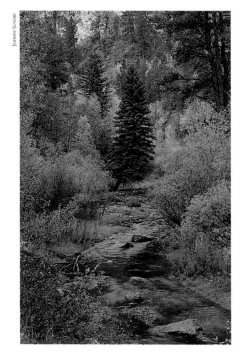

JOHNNY SUNDBY

SPEARFISH CREEK winds its way through fall foliage in colorful Spearfish Canyon.

THE last light of day touches the tops of the Cathedral Spires as viewed from the summit of Harney Peak.

JOHNNY SUNDBY

JOHNNY SUNDBY

SOUTH DAKOTA'S state flower, the pasque, blooms in early spring throughout the Black Hills.

JOHNNY SUNDBY

MOVING clouds paint brush-strokes across the midnight sky.

JOHN A. SUNDBY

IN the quiet of winter, snow dusts
the serene Cathedral Spires.

JOHN SUNDBY

THE bronze waters by the Pactola shoreline create a patterned ta-
pestry at sunset.

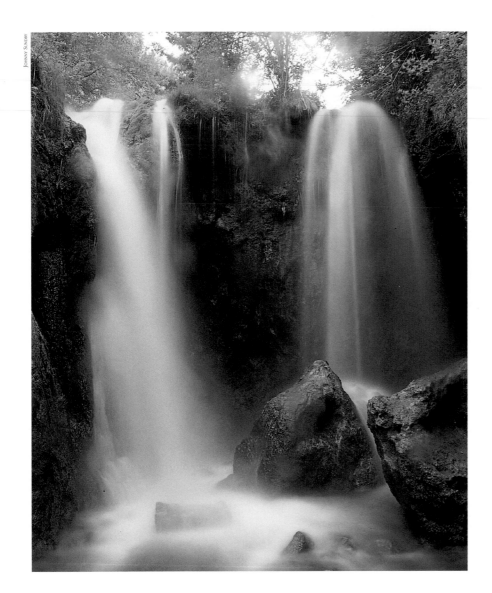

WATER cascades over Roughlock Falls in Spearfish Canyon at Savoy.

SEDIMENT from an ancient sea forms the limestone walls of Spearfish Canyon in this view from the Latchstring Village at Savoy.

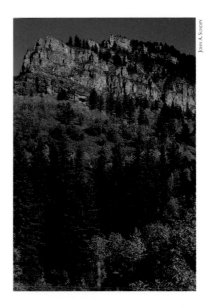

D EVILS TOWER, in the north-
western corner of the Black Hills, is
believed by some geologists to be
the core of an ancient under-
ground volcano. It was the film site
for the movie "Close Encounters
of the Third Kind."

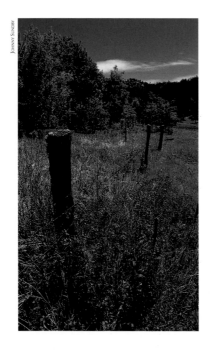

JOHNNY SUNDBY

W ILDFLOWERS in a myriad of
hues bloom each summer in the
Black Hills.

JOHNNY SUNDBY

A boulder bathes in the mist
of Roughlock Falls.

JOHNNY SUNDBY

JOHNNY SUNDBY

AN Easter morning sunrise
warms the South Dakota sky as
viewed from Highway 16.

W<small>INTER</small> transforms Spearfish
Creek into a tranquil Christmas
card scene.

W<small>IND</small> C<small>AVE</small> is famous for its
boxwork, which forms when min-
erals crystallize in softer rock,
which later dissolves.

A splash of sunflowers paints the arid landscape of the Badlands west of Cedar Pass.

D EVILS TOWER National Monument pierces a sapphire sky.

JOHNNY SUNDBY

A silken stream weaves through Spearfish Canyon.

JOHNNY SUNDBY

A lone rider returns home
after a last check over his herd
east of Rapid City.

SPECTATORS enjoy a kaleidoscope of colors at the annual Elks Club Balloon Rally in Rapid City.

JOHNNY SUNDBY

JOHNNY SUNDBY

A ranger hangs on the stone eyelash of Thomas Jefferson on Mount Rushmore patching cracks. Each year, cracks are filled with a silicone building material to retard erosion.

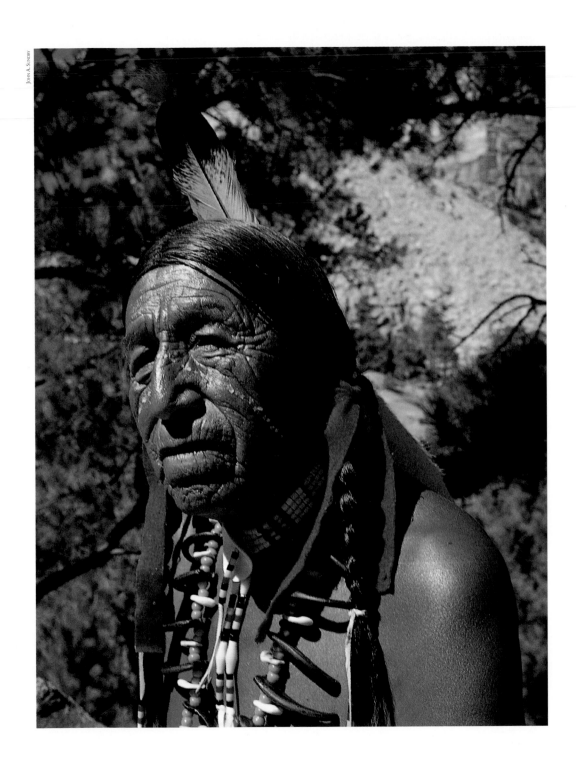

BEN BLACK ELK, was photographed by millions of Mount Rushmore visitors from the 1940's until his death in 1972. Ben was the grandson of Oglala Sioux holy man Black Elk.

JOHNNY SUNDBY

A horse and rider step gingerly into the frigid December waters in Dark Canyon west of Rapid City.

A hot air balloon drifts quietly above the Shrine of Democracy.

Cowboys on the Pine Ridge Indian Reservation finish the day's chores.

A young Lakota fancy dancer becomes a swirl of colors at the "Come Dance With Us" powwow in Rapid City.

AFTER leaping from his horse,
a bulldogger wrestles a steer,
easily twice the cowboy's weight,
at the All-Indian Crazy Horse
Stampede Rodeo.

JOHNNY SUNDBY

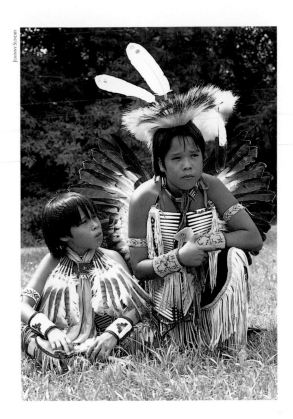

JOHNNY SUNDBY

Two young Lakota brothers think about the upcoming competition as they await their chance to dance at a Central States Fair pow-wow in Rapid City.

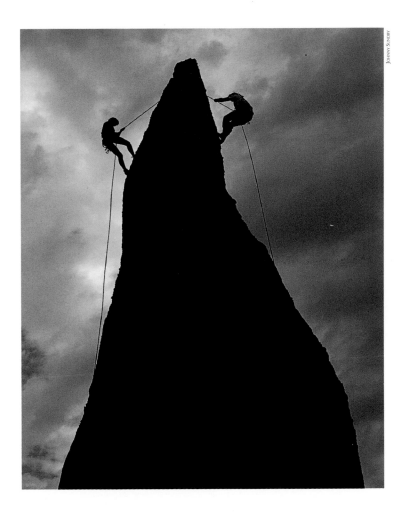

JOHNNY SUNDBY

Two climbers counterweight each other as they descend a granite spire in the Needles.

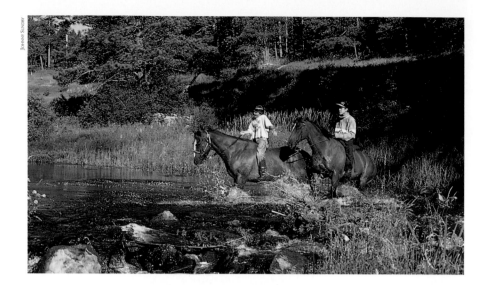

YOUNG horseback riders splash through Box Elder Creek at the Nemo Guest Ranch.

BUNGEE JUMPERS place their trust in God and in a high-tech harness and cord system when freefalling over 10 stories.

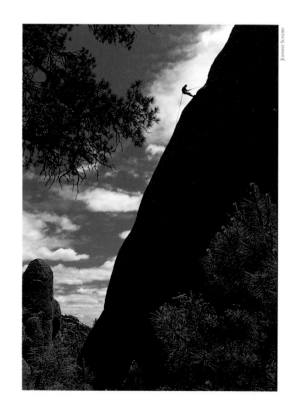

A rock climber rappels off a granite spire near Mount Rushmore.

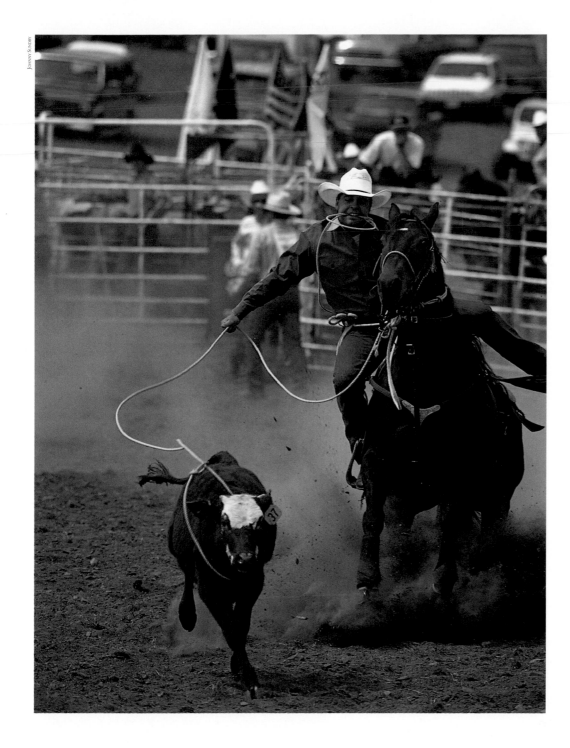

PRACTICAL ranch skills have evolved into the West's popular sport of rodeo. Today professional cowboys make a living winning money on the rodeo circuit.

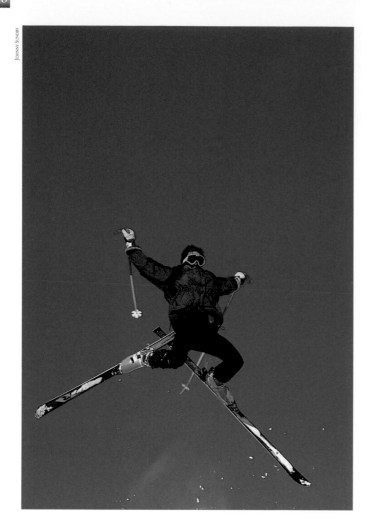

A skier soars into an azure sky at Terry Peak Ski Area, one of two ski areas near Lead in the Northern Hills.

A young cowboy practices his roping skills at the South Dakota High School Finals Rodeo in Sturgis.

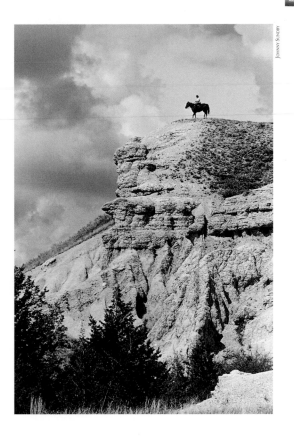

JOHNNY SUNDBY

A Pine Ridge rancher surveys goings-on at a large ranch south of Interior.

A An ice climber rappels down frozen Bridal Veil Falls in Spearfish Canyon.

JOHNNY SUNDBY

JOHNNY SUNDBY

A Lakota Sioux man enjoys the company of relatives and friends during the weekend festivities at the Veterans Powwow at Pine Ridge village .

JOHNNY SUNDBY

Each spring ranchers brand their calves to prevent cattle rustling.

JOHNNY SUNDBY

A tunnel on Iron Mountain Road frames the faces of Mount Rushmore.

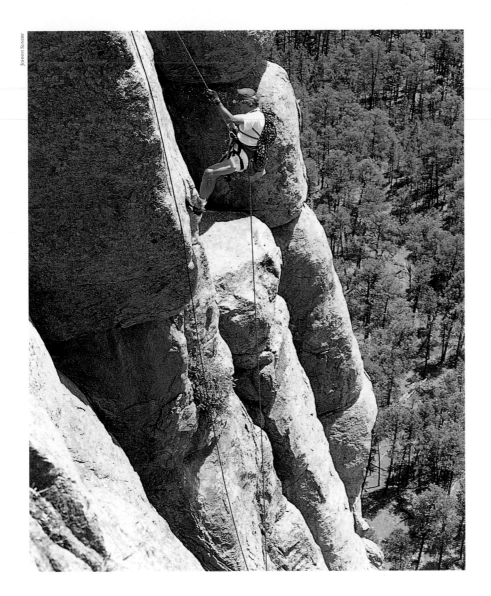

JOHNNY SUNDBY

A climber rappels down the massive columns of Devils Tower. Since 1937, when records were first kept, over 28,000 climbers have scaled the 867 feet to its summit. The first ascent was in 1893.

A snowboarder catches some "big air" off a cliff at Deer Mountain Ski Area.

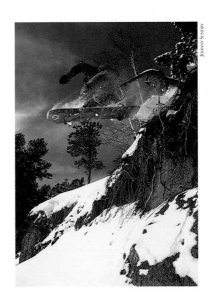

JOHNNY SUNDBY

Sculptor Gutzon Borglum
carved Mount Rushmore from
1927 until his death in 1941.
Each head is approximately
six stories tall.

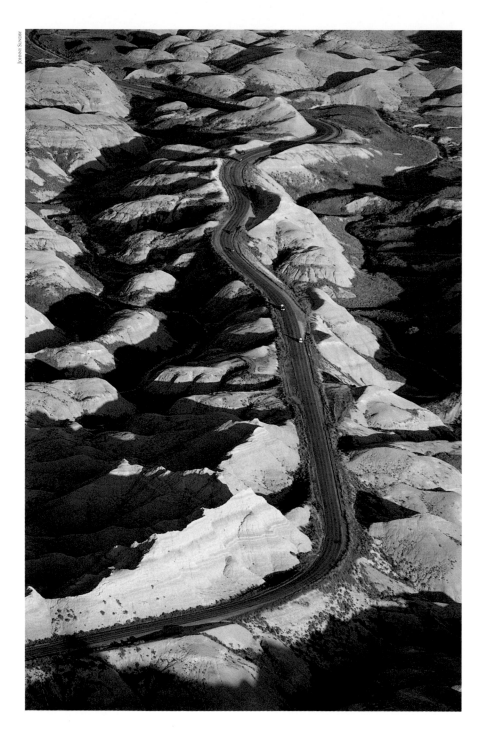

JOHNNY SUNDBY

THE Badlands Loop Road snakes across the parched spine of Badlands National Park's western edge.

JOHN A. SUNDBY

IRISES grow where children once played near a schoolhouse in the turn-of-the-century mining town of Spokane, located close to Iron Mountain Road. Numerous metals, including gold and silver, were mined there.

JOHNNY SUNDBY

OPEN year-round, the Shrine of Democracy attracts over 2 million visitors annually.

TAIL lights streak over Highway 244 behind Mount Rushmore at dusk.

HOARFROST clings to an old wagon on a ranch near Rockerville.

JOHNNY SUNDBY

WEEDS stretch toward a wind-

mill near Hermosa.

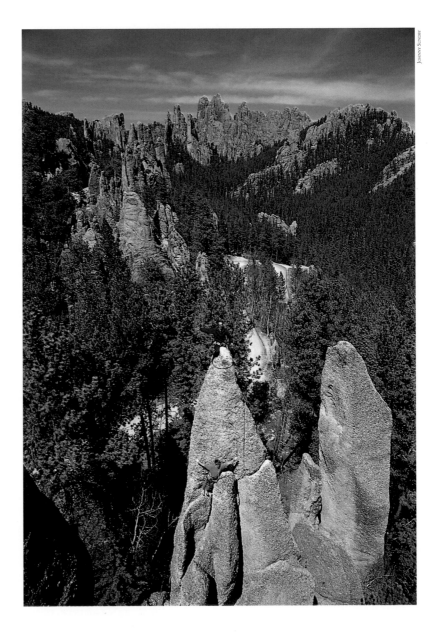

JOHNNY SUNDBY

BLACK HILLS climbers enjoy

the vista from Tent Peg Spire

in the Needles.

THE historic Finnish Church in Lead rests on blocks prior to being moved to accommodate the growth of Homestake's Open Cut mine.

BUILT on the Chicago, Burlington & Quincy Railroad line in 1889, this tall trestle between Custer and Hill City carried trains across the gorge for 94 years. In the mid 1970s, the 1880 Train crossed the bridge after flood waters washed out the Hill City to Keystone route.

AT 7,242 feet above sea level, Harney Peak is the highest peak east of the Rockies in the United States. The stone building on the summit was built by the Civilian Conservation Corps in 1938-39 and was a manned fire tower for over 30 years.

JOHNNY SUNDBY

AT MEMORIAL LAKE, named for the victims who died in the 1972 Rapid City Flood, one's spirit can reflect along with the rising sun.

THE faces of Mount Rushmore glow under a July moon during the lighting ceremony held each summer evening at the memorial.

JOHNNY SUNDBY

Rising 1,200 feet above the prairie, Bear Butte is considered sacred by Native Americans who still come here to pray.

Changing aspen trees line the narrow and twisting Iron Mountain Road near Keystone.

JOHN A. SUNDBY

THE face of Thomas Jefferson was originally carved into the granite at George Washington's right. Due to unsuitable rock, the face was blasted off the mountain and carved to Washington's left.

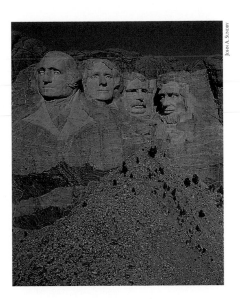

NEEDLES Highway winds through granite spires, the core of an ancient Black Hills that once stretched nearly as high as the much younger Rockies.

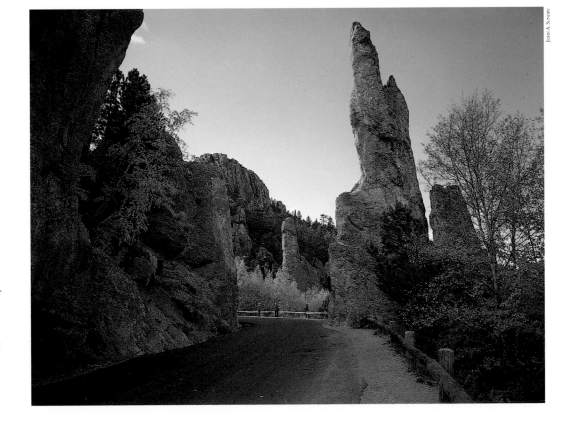

JOHN A. SUNDBY

THE 5 a.m. sunrise illumi-
nates a grain elevator in Cotton-
wood as the full moon drops
into the horizon.

JOHNNY SUNDBY

QUAKING golden aspen leaves frame the faces of George Washington, Thomas Jefferson, Theodore Roosevelt, and Abraham Lincoln.

JOHNNY SUNDBY

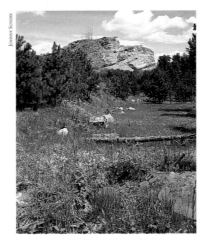

JOHNNY SUNDBY

IN the southern Black Hills, Lakota leader Crazy Horse is emerging as the world's largest sculpture. Sculptor Korczak Ziolkowski (1908-1982) began the non-profit project at the invitation of Lakota chiefs.

A touch of cowboy humor is displayed in the worn boots that top fence posts along Highway 16 west of Custer.

IN any season, Mount Rushmore is spectacular. A unique side view is obtained by driving Highway 244 behind the memorial toward Hill City.

JOHN A. SUNDBY

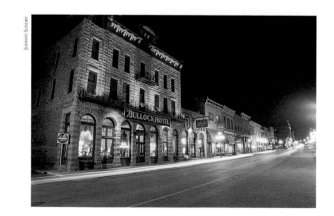

JOHNNY SUNDBY

HISTORIC Deadwood, once home to Calamity Jane and Wild Bill Hickok, offers round-the-clock gambling, dining and dancing.

WILDFLOWERS blanket a field in front of a dilapidated barn south of Lead.

LIGHTNING cracks the night sky over Rapid City.

A helicopter provides a dramatic panorama of the Badlands east entrance.

JOHNNY SUNDBY

UNDER the midnight moon, dinosaurs still appear to rule the earth at Dinosaur Park in Rapid City.

JOHN A. SUNDBY

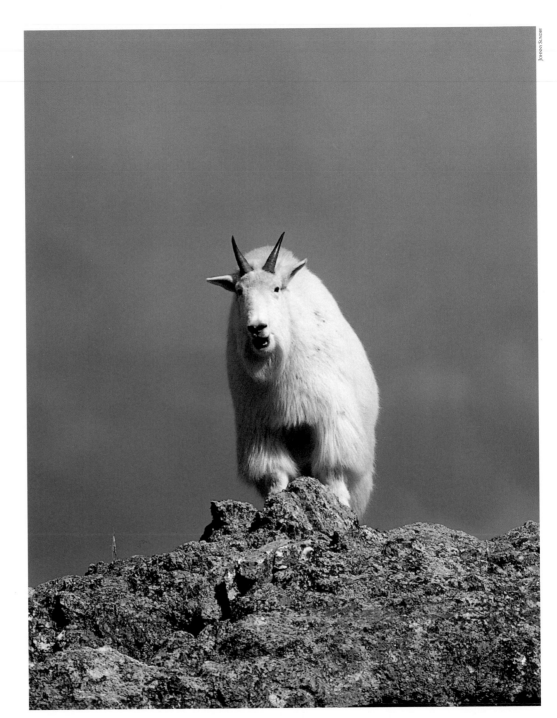

JOHNNY SUNDBY

SINCE their introduction into Custer State Park in 1924 from Canada, mountain goats have migrated and thrived in several areas of the Black Hills including the Mount Rushmore area.

A bison calf, less than one day old, takes its first steps on wobbly legs as its mother keeps a watchful eye.

JOHNNY SUNDBY

JOHNNY SUNDBY

PRONGHORN ANTELOPE, which can reach speeds of up to 50 miles per hour, are the fastest land animals in North America.

UNDER a full moon, a bull elk holds his ground on Boland Ridge in Wind Cave National Park.

JOHNNY SUNDBY

JOHNNY SUNDBY

A bison bull forages his way up a gully in the Badlands where thousands of his ancestors once roamed before the arrival of the "wasichu" or white man.

ABOUT 40 turkeys roost in a
leafless treetop near Hermosa
dispelling the myth that turkeys
cannot fly.

JOHNNY SUNDBY

BEAR cubs frolic at Bear
Country U.S.A., one of several
tourist attractions on Highway
16 south of Rapid City.

A large coil of rattlesnake
sounds its warning with a nervous
twitching of its tail.

JOHNNY SUNDBY

JOHNNY SUNDBY

CUSTER STATE PARK bison amble toward the park's buffalo corrals during the annual, fall roundup.

SCREECH OWLETS in a Rapid City park watch and wait for their mother to return.

JOHNNY SUNDBY

A bull elk bugles on a ridge at Wind Cave National Park at sunset during the fall rut.

HARDIER than cattle, Custer State Park bison rest while the snow falls.

HUNTERS from many states come to western South Dakota each fall in search of trophies like this prize whitetail buck.

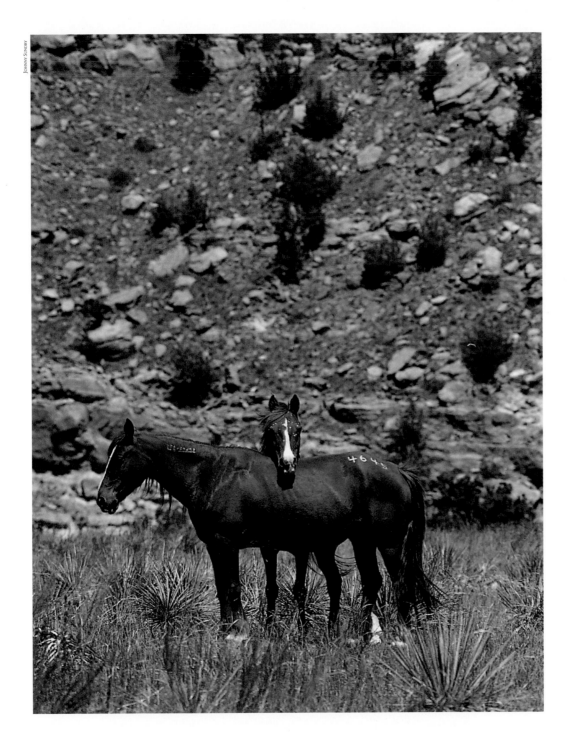

JOHNNY SUNDBY

A young mare peeks shyly over her mother's back at the Black Hills Wild Horse Sanctuary, south of Hot Springs.

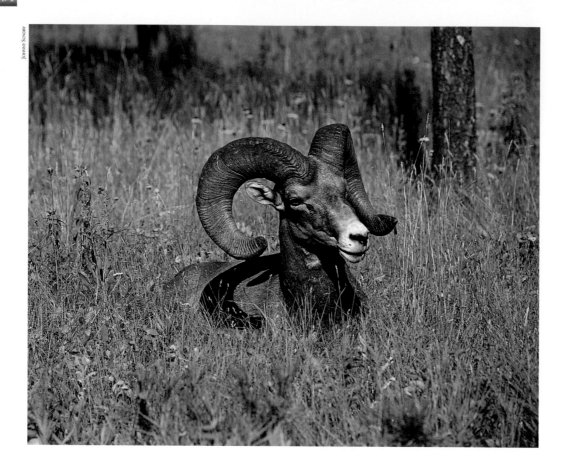

JOHNNY SUNDBY

CURLED horns frame the face of a bighorn sheep resting in a meadow of wildflowers in Custer State Park.

IN the golden glow of first light, antelope graze on a grassy flat near Badlands National Park.